BEST BUDS
TOGETHER FUN

by Jake Black

An Imprint of Penguin Random House

CARTOON NETWORK BOOKS
Penguin Young Readers Group
An Imprint of Penguin Random House LLC

Cover and additional illustrations by Shane L. Johnson

Published in 2016 by Cartoon Network Books, an imprint of Penguin Random House LLC.
345 Hudson Street, New York, New York 10014.
Manufactured in China.

ISBN 978-1-101-99516-7   10 9 8 7 6 5 4 3 2 1

WELCOME!

We are the Crystal Gems, and we're here to protect the world—especially Beach City. But we need your help! This book will prepare you to join us in our heroic adventures. You might not have Gem powers, but that doesn't mean you can't be a hero! After all, it takes a team to save the world. So let's get together and have some fun adventures. And remember: "If every pork chop were perfect, we wouldn't have hot dogs!"

TABLE OF CONTENTS

Who Are You?

If you want to become an honorary Crystal Gem, we need to know a little about you first. Answer the questions below, so we can get to know you better and help you join the Crystal Gems' mission.

What is your name?

Do you believe in magic?

Do you think creatures from other planets are friendly or dangerous?

How many people are in your family?

Who is your best friend?

What do you want to be when you grow up?

Where do you live?

What is your favorite color?

Gem Selection

Now we need to figure out your Gem. Check out the list below, and see what your birthstone is, based on the month you were born. Circle the correct month for you!

January—Garnet

February—Amethyst

March—Aquamarine

April—Diamond

May—Emerald

June—Pearl or Alexandrite

July—Ruby

August—Peridot

September—Sapphire

October—Opal or Tourmaline

November—Topaz

December—Turquoise

GEM CUTOUTS!

How would you like some sweet Crystal Gems to play with or display? Using safety scissors, cut out each Gem and stand on the following pages. Then cut out their phrases and stands, and you can pretend that they're training you, going on an adventure, or just hanging out at home.

Some of us are trying to protect humanity.

I am pretty great!

Chill it, dude.

Don't hold back!

I am pretty great!

Some of us are trying to protect humanity.

Don't hold back!

Chill it, dude.

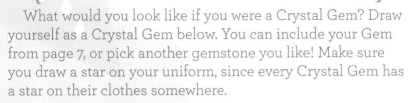

Your Gem Look

What would you look like if you were a Crystal Gem? Draw yourself as a Crystal Gem below. You can include your Gem from page 7, or pick another gemstone you like! Make sure you draw a star on your uniform, since every Crystal Gem has a star on their clothes somewhere.

Gem Fusion

Crystal Gems can join together to become a more powerful Gem. This is called Fusion. Garnet is actually a Fusion of two other Gems. If you could join together with someone else to become more powerful, who would it be? Why would you choose that person (or those people)?

Fusion Confusion

Draw a line from each pair to their Fusion.

A. Alexandrite

D. Opal

1. Pearl and Amethyst

2. Garnet and Amethyst

3. Steven and Connie

4. Ruby and Sapphire

5. Garnet, Pearl, and Amethyst

6. Pearl and Garnet

B. Stevonnie

E. Sugilite

C. Garnet

F. Sardonyx

Garnet Quiz

Think you know Garnet?
Take this quiz and prove it!

1. Garnet uses which weapon?
a) Sword
b) Shield
c) Gauntlets
d) Whip

2. Which of the following is one of Garnet's powers?
a) Future vision
b) Healing
c) Time travel
d) Super speed

3. How many eyes does Garnet have?
a) 1
b) 2
c) 3
d) 4

4. Garnet is a Fusion of which two Gems?
a) Turquoise and Ruby
b) Ruby and Sapphire
c) Sapphire and Turquoise
d) Ruby and Peridot

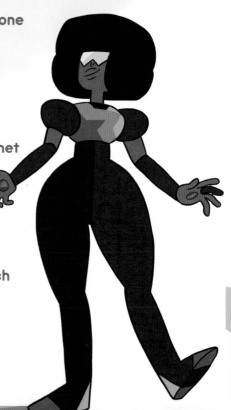

Pearl Quiz

What do you know about Pearl? She's a Crystal Gem, obviously. But what else do you know? Take the quiz below to show off your amazing Pearl knowledge.

1. What is Pearl's weapon?
a) Shield
b) Gauntlets
c) Boxing gloves
d) Spear

2. Which of these is one of Pearl's special abilities?
a) Making holographic projections
b) Creating hot blue fire
c) Reading humans' minds
d) Repairing warp pads

3. How old is Pearl?
a) 1,000 years
b) 35 years
c) Several thousand years
d) Newborn

4. Which style of dance does Pearl do during Fusion?
a) Hip-hop
b) Ballet
c) Tap dancing
d) Salsa

Amethyst Quiz

Amethyst is funky and spunky.
We dare you to take this quiz about her!

1. What is Amethyst's weapon of choice?
    a) Nunchakus
    b) Whip
    c) Sword
    d) Shield

2. What was Amethyst's professional wrestling name?
    a) Purple Powerhouse
    b) Purple Puma
    c) Purple Pummeler
    d) Purple Meanie

3. Which word best describes Amethyst's room?
    a) Cloudy
    b) Tidy
    c) Dry
    d) Messy

4. Where was Amethyst "born"?
    a) Gem Homeworld
    b) The ocean
    c) The Gem "Kindergarten" on Earth
    d) A spaceship heading to Earth

STEVEN QUIZ

Steven Universe is the youngest Crystal Gem, but he's still an important part of the team! Find out how much you know about Steven with this quiz.

1. Which of these can Steven summon with his Gem power?
- a) His singing voice
- b) Extra muscles
- c) Shield
- d) Cookie Cats

2. Which Gem is Steven's mother?
- a) Rose Quartz
- b) Garnet
- c) Pearl
- d) Amethyst

3. Which musical instrument does Steven play?
- a) Harmonica
- b) Ukulele
- c) Accordion
- d) Saxophone

4. What was the name of Steven's rock band?
- a) Rolling Gem Stones
- b) Steven and the Stevens
- c) The Stevees
- d) REO Steve Wagon

REHOBOTH BAY
BEACH CITY WATERTOWER
BEACH CITY
THE MAYOR'S HOUSE
1A
TOWARD
13
95
FUNLAND AMUSEMENT PARK
THE OLD DOCKS (DESTROYED)
U-STOR SELF STORAGE
IT'S A WASH
DEWEY PARK
BEACH CITY VISITOR CENTER
CONE 'N' SON
FUNLAND ARCADE
BEACH CITYWALK FRIES
FISH STEW PIZZA
???
T-SHIRT SHOP
THE BIG DONUT
BEACH CITY
DELMARVA

Welcome to Beach City!

Steven and the Gems live here and protect it from danger. There are a lot of awesome places to go and people to see. If you were to visit Beach City, what places would you be sure to visit? Mark each one with an X, so you'll remember to go there on your next trip!

THE BITS! THE BITS!

Steven is obsessed with getting fry bits at Beach Citywalk Fries. Guide him through the maze so he can get some bits, but be quick—he's hungry, and a guy's gotta get his fry bits on!

VIP(izza) Only

One of the most popular places to hang out in Beach City is Fish Stew Pizza, where you can order whatever kinds of toppings you want on your pizza. What would you order? Draw your favorite kind of pizza on the plate above.

KEEP BEACH CITY WEIRD

Ronaldo Fryman runs a blog talking about all the weird stuff and conspiracies that go on in Beach City. I bet weird stuff goes on in your hometown, too. In the space provided, write it all down!

Name of my town:

....

....

I heard something weird happened at:

....

....

It was:

....

....

....

....

....

I think that's:

....

....

I hope the next weird thing to happen will be:

....

....

It all makes me feel:

....

....

The best thing about living here is:

....

....

The worst thing about living in this town is:

....

....

My favorite place in my hometown is:

....

....

Because:

....

....

Do or Do Nut

Welcome to your job interview at the Big Donut.
Answer the questions on the next page honestly, and
we'll see if you're qualified to work here with us!

EMPLOYMENT APPLICATION

1. Why would you want to work at the Big Donut?
- a) Free donuts
- b) I like helping customers
- c) More free donuts
- d) All of the above

2. What's your favorite kind of donut?
- a) Chocolate frosted
- b) Sprinkles
- c) Maple bar
- d) Other _____

3. If alien space monsters were to attack the shop, what would you do?
- a) Run away
- b) Cry
- c) Fight them off myself, single-handedly saving the day
- d) Call for Steven Universe and the Crystal Gems to save me

4. Which drink goes best with a donut?
- a) Water
- b) Milk
- c) Hot chocolate
- d) Orange juice

5. How many donuts can you eat in one sitting?
- a) Less than 1
- b) 1–3
- c) 4–6
- d) A full dozen

6. Donuts are best served
- a) For breakfast
- b) As a treat during school
- c) For dinner
- d) Anytime

7. What is the best non-donut treat served at the Big Donut?
- a) Lion Lickers ice cream
- b) Cupcakes
- c) Spicy pretzels
- d) None of these. Bring back Cookie Cats!

8. Describe a new donut you would invent.

_____
_____
_____
_____
_____

ARCADE MANIA

The games at Funland Arcade are totally wicked. Design your amazing video game that will become the hottest game EVER at Funland! Be sure to give it an exciting title, too!

The U Stor

Steven's dad, Greg, has a tightly packed storage unit at the U Stor facility in town. There, he keeps all his possessions that he can't fit into his van. Find and circle the items listed below.

- **Portrait of Rose Quartz**
- **Videotapes of the TV show** *Li'l Butler*
- **A large TV**
- **The Laser Light Cannon**
- **Comic books**
- **Golf clubs**
- **A guitar**
- **A Mr. Universe record album**

Who's Who: Human Edition

How familiar are you with the Boardies?
Check out their pictures and write their names
on the lines. If you need help, check the clue
that accompanies each picture.

1. He's Steven's dad.

2. She's Steven's
best friend.

- - - - - - - - - - -   - - - - - - - - - - -

3. He cooks Steven's
favorite food—bits.

- - - - - - - - - - -

4. He owns the Funland arcade.

5. He steals stuff sometimes.

- - - - - - - - - - - -   - - - - - - - - - - - -

6. He's the mayor of Beach City.

7. Her family owns Fish Stew Pizza.

- - - - - - - - - - - -   - - - - - - - - - - - -

8. He wants to be one of the cool kids.

9. She is Steven's best friend's mom.

- - - - - - - - - - - - -　　- - - - - - - - - - - - -

10. He used to have to dress up as Frybo.

11. He's the mayor's popular son.

- - - - - - - - - - - - -　　- - - - - - - - - - - - -

12. He is very protective of his daughter.

- - - - - - - - - - - - -

13. He delivers the mail.

- - - - - - - - - - - - -

14. He owns Fish Stew Pizza.

- - - - - - - - - - - - -

15. She works at the Big Donut.

- - - - - - - - - - - - -

Connie Quiz

Connie is Steven's best friend. Do you know her as well as Steven does? Take the quiz below to find out.

1. What sport does Connie play?
 a) Football
 b) Volleyball
 c) Tennis
 d) Rugby

2. Why does Connie not need to wear her glasses anymore (even though she still does)?
 a) Steven healed her eyes with his saliva.
 b) Pearl used special Gem magic to fix her eyes.
 c) She got laser eye surgery.
 d) She never needed to wear them to begin with.

3. Which musical instrument does Connie play?
 a) Flute
 b) Guitar
 c) Harp
 d) Violin

4. What was Steven and Connie's first adventure together?
 a) Trapped in a bubble together
 b) Fused together into Stevonnie
 c) Orbited Earth in a homemade spaceship
 d) Escaped capture by evil Gems

Greg Quiz

Steven's dad, Greg, is a pretty simple guy. But is this quiz about him just as simple?

1. Where does Greg live?
a) In a beach house
b) With Steven and the Gems
c) In his van
d) In his storage unit at U Stor

2. What was the name of Greg's hit song from his rock band?
a) "Can You Hear Me Now?"
b) "Let Me Drive My Van (into Your Heart)"
c) "If Every Pork Chop Were Perfect"
d) "We Are the Crystal Gems"

3. Which Beach City business does Greg own?
a) Fish Stew Pizza
b) The Big Donut
c) Funland Arcade
d) It's a Wash car wash

4. What did Greg help Pearl build?
a) A laboratory
b) A swimming pool
c) A spaceship
d) A house

MR. UNIVERSE

Greg wrote a song that won Rose Quartz's heart. Try your hand at writing a killer song!

VILLAIN CUTOUTS

The Gems need foes to battle! Using safety scissors, cut out each villain and stand on the following pages. Then cut out their phrases and stands, and you can pretend that they're battling the Crystal Gems or trying to destroy the world.

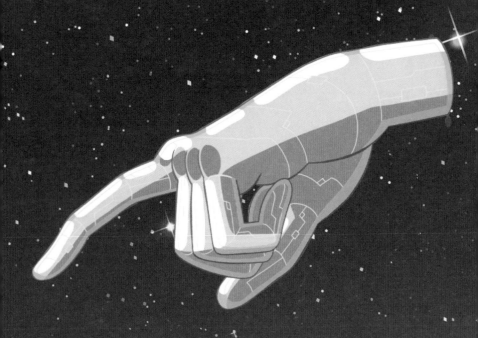

They're the ones that keep breaking my machines!

You clods don't know what you're doing!

Why are you so weak?

I'm tired of being everyone's prisoner. Now you're my prisoner, and I'm never letting you go!

You clods don't know what you're doing!

They're the ones that keep breaking my machines!

I'm tired of being everyone's prisoner. Now you're my prisoner, and I'm never letting you go!

Why are you so weak?

IMPORTANT MESSAGE!

Gems from the Gem Homeworld are planning another attack on Earth, and you intercepted their secret plans. Write out the plans so you can inform the Crystal Gems what their enemies are going to do!

....

....

....

....

....

....

....

....

....

....

....

....

....

FEAR FACTOR

The Crystal Gems battle a lot of scary creatures, like monsters and Homeworld Gems. Everyone is scared of something. Describe something that you're afraid of below, and then draw a terrifying monster in the space provided on the next page.

....

....

....

....

....

....

....

....

....

....

....

Mirror Gem

Lapis Lazuli was trapped in a magic mirror for many years. Maybe there's another Gem trapped in this one. Draw that Gem, and tell its story in the space provided on the next page.

What is the Gem's name?

_____

Where was this trapped Gem from?

_____

_____

How did the Gem get trapped in the mirror?

_____

_____

_____

_____

_____

Will you free this Gem from the mirror?

Why or why not?

_____

_____

_____

What questions do you want to ask the mirror?

_____

_____

Who's Who: Villain Edition

How familiar are you with the enemies that force the Crystal Gems into battle? Check out their pictures and write their names on the lines. If you need help, check the clue that accompanies each picture.

1. She fought Garnet on the Gem Warship.

_ _ _ _ _ _ _ _ _ _ _ _

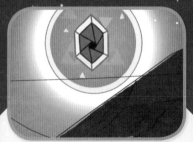

2. She was trapped in a mirror.

_ _ _ _ _ _ _ _ _ _ _ _

3. It looks like what its name is.

_ _ _ _ _ _ _ _ _ _ _ _

4. She repairs warp pads.

_ _ _ _ _ _ _ _ _ _ _ _

5. It's a cold-hearted
creature.

_ _ _ _ _ _ _ _ _ _ _

6. It's an inflatable
undersea creature.

_ _ _ _ _ _ _ _ _ _ _

7. Steven imagined this
character in Garnet's world.

_ _ _ _ _ _ _ _ _ _ _ _

8. He's a restaurant
mascot turned evil.

_ _ _ _ _ _ _ _ _ _ _

9. It's sort of like an Earth
insect, but much grosser.

_ _ _ _ _ _ _ _ _ _ _

10. It only *looks* like a
Crystal Gem.

_ _ _ _ _ _ _ _ _ _ _

FAVORITE POSSESSIONS

Everyone has a favorite possession. In the space beneath each picture, write the name of the person that object belongs to or the person who uses it the most.

1.

2.

3.

4.

5.

6.

7.

8.

9.

10.

Warp Pad Connections

Warp pads can send a Gem from place to place almost instantly, and there are a lot of them spread throughout the universe. Play this game with a friend. Each player takes a turn connecting the warp pads below, one line at a time, to make a square. (The lines should be horizontal or vertical, not diagonal.) When you complete your square, put your initials in it. Then you get to take another turn. You can use your opponent's lines to make squares. Once all the squares have been made, the player who made the most squares wins!

Packing for Backpacking

Steven's cheeseburger backpack is a very useful tool. He carries all the supplies he needs for adventures—including snacks. He must not forget the snacks! What do you carry in your backpack? Write a list below!

What's the Difference?

When protecting the world from evil, it's very important that you have perfect observation skills. Practice that by examining these two pictures and spotting the differences. Draw a circle around each difference you find.

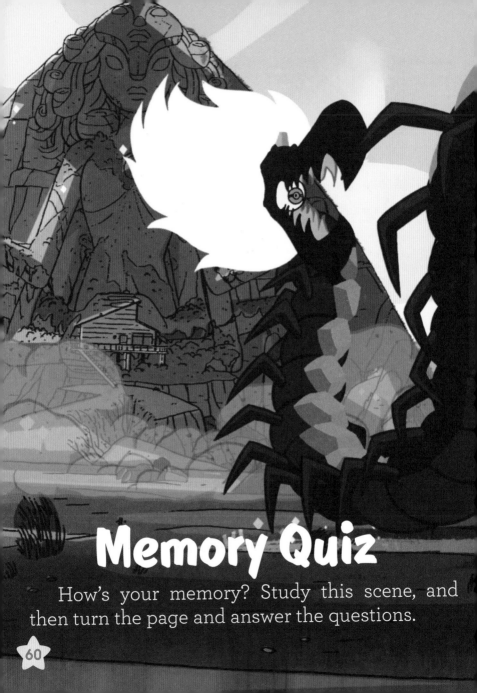

Memory Quiz

How's your memory? Study this scene, and then turn the page and answer the questions.

Okay, you think you're ready? You memorized the scene on the previous pages? Answer the questions below. But remember, NO PEEKING!

1. How many members of the Crystal Gems are pictured?

....

2. What colors are Pearl's clothes?

....

3. What weapons are the Gems using?

....

4. Who are they battling?

....

5. What is Steven doing?

....

6. Which Crystal Gem is farthest to the right?

....

7. Is it daytime or nighttime?

....

8. What color is the monster's hair?

....

9. Where is the scene taking place?

....

10. Are any Gem Fusions in the picture?

....

PARTY TIME!

With your training complete, you're ready to go on adventures with the Crystal Gems! But first let's celebrate your training success with a party!

When is the party?

Where is the party?

Who will you invite?

What food will you eat?

What activities will you do?

How should people dress for the party?

What gifts do you hope they bring?

GEM ADVENTURE

Tell your own Crystal Gem story! Draw and write a Steven Universe comic on the following pages!

69

Race to the Temple

Play this game with a friend, using pennies as game pieces. Place your pennies at the *Steven Universe* starting space, and take turns moving around the game board. On your turn, flip a coin—move ahead two spaces for heads, one space for tails. The first player to make it to the Temple wins.

START

Find Cookie Cats at the store. JUMP AHEAD ONE SPACE.

Lose some of your GUYS. GO BACK ONE SPACE.

Win singing contest at Beach-A-Palooza. JUMP AHEAD ONE SPACE.

You made it! You are the first one home to the Temple after completing your adventure! **YOU WIN!**

Escape from your homemade spaceship as it falls apart. **GO BACK THREE SPACES.**

Use a warp pad to travel. **JUMP AHEAD TWO SPACES.**

Attacked by clones of yourself. **GO BACK ONE SPACE.**

Fuse with the other Gems. **JUMP AHEAD ONE SPACE.**

GARNET'S UNIVERSE

Garnet has just returned from a mission. She doesn't want to talk about it, so Steven is making up what he thinks happened on her mission. Help him by filling in the appropriate words on this page, and adding them to the story on the next page.

1. TYPE OF FOOD _____

2. VERB (PAST TENSE) _____

3. ADVERB _____

4. A PLACE _____

5. NOUN _____

6. EMOTION _____

7. VERB _____

8. VERB (PAST TENSE) _____

9. EMOTION _____

10. VERB (PAST TENSE) _____

11. NOUN _____

12. VERB (PAST TENSE) _____

13. FAMOUS PHRASE _____

This morning, you got up early and ate _____
TYPE OF FOOD

for breakfast. Then you _____ on the
VERB (PAST TENSE)

warp pad and traveled very _____ to (the)
ADVERB

_____. There you saw a giant Gem creature that
A PLACE

looked like a/an _____. It made you feel really
NOUN

_____. So you decided to _____ it.
EMOTION   VERB

The Gem _____ back at you. That
VERB (PAST TENSE)

made you _____, so you _____ a/an
EMOTION   VERB (PAST TENSE)

_____ and _____ at the Gem monster.
NOUN   VERB (PAST TENSE)

It ran away. As it left, you said, "_____."
FAMOUS PHRASE

Word Search!

Check out the word search. Look up, down, diagonally, forward, and backward to find the words listed below!

AMETHYST
BACKPACK
BEACH CITY
BITS
COOKIE CATS

CRYSTAL GEMS
FRYBO
FUNLAND
GARNET
JASPER

LAPIS LAZULI
PEARL
PERIDOT
STEVEN
UKULELE

T	O	C	L	B	R	E	S	E	O	B	S	W	C	Z
F	S	B	Y	A	P	D	L	T	E	C	T	P	O	L
M	J	B	Y	N	P	E	E	A	E	J	I	E	O	H
U	M	V	R	R	L	I	C	B	A	V	B	U	K	R
A	O	B	F	U	F	H	S	S	B	X	E	A	I	T
Y	N	I	K	I	C	B	P	L	A	J	Q	N	E	O
T	D	U	D	I	L	E	M	N	A	M	C	R	C	D
V	S	C	T	X	R	S	T	S	B	Z	H	C	A	I
C	R	Y	S	T	A	L	G	E	M	S	U	T	T	R
G	B	I	H	D	D	N	D	F	S	Q	Q	L	S	E
A	O	Q	K	T	C	H	G	J	C	X	A	R	I	P
R	N	Q	V	G	E	F	U	N	L	A	N	D	C	O
N	L	R	A	E	P	M	N	C	W	J	R	F	I	Z
E	L	K	G	W	D	P	A	H	B	L	C	R	F	I
T	P	X	K	C	A	P	K	C	A	B	V	C	V	Y

Coded Message

Sometimes, when you're on an adventure, you need to send a coded message to the other people on your adventure. Using the key below, decode this message.

A=Z	E=V	I=R	M=N	Q=J	U=F	Y=B
B=Y	F=U	J=Q	N=M	R=I	V=E	Z=A
C=X	G=T	K=P	O=L	S=H	W=D	
D=W	H=S	L=O	P=K	T=G	X=C	

Dv zodzbh hzev gsv wzb!

__ __ _____ _____ ____

____ ___!

Status Updates

Social media is popular everywhere, even in Beach City! Write some status updates (descriptions of activities they're currently doing) or deep thoughts each character is having in the space provided beneath their social media page!

 Steven Quartz Universe • 1m

↩   ⇄   ★   • • •

 Garnet • 4m

↩   ⇄   ★ 4   • • •

 Pearl • 5m

↩   ⇄ 1   ★ 1   • • •

 Amethyst • 8m

↩   ⇄ 3   ★   • • •

 Steven Quartz Universe • 14m

↩   ⇄ 6   ★   • • •

Ronaldo Fryman · 20m

_____

↩ ⇄ ★ 2 · · ·

Greg Universe · 22m

_____

↩ ⇄ ★ 3 · · ·

Connie Maheswaran · 26m

_____

↩ ⇄ 2 ★ · · ·

Pearl · 30m

_____

↩ ⇄ ★ · · ·

Amethyst · 32m

_____

↩ ⇄ 1 ★ 2 · · ·

Ronaldo Fryman · 45m

_____

↩ ⇄ ★ · · ·

Coloring Time!

Using pencils, pens, crayons, markers, or whatever, color the scene below! You can make it "authentic" by flipping through this book to see what everyone usually looks like, or you can be creative and color it however you want. No matter what, just have fun coloring this epic adventure!

The Write Stuff

After an epic adventure, Steven likes to write down what happened in his journal. What adventures did you have today? Write them down in the space below.

_____

_____

_____

_____

_____

_____

_____

_____

_____

_____

_____

_____

_____

_____

Home Sweet Home

The Crystal Gems live in the amazing Temple. This place has everything! Waterfalls, fire pits, trapped Gem monsters, pink clouds—EVERYTHING! Steven lives in a beach house right next to the Temple, and he loves living there. What is your dream house like? Draw it below. Make sure you include all the awesome features you want—like a moat or laser cannons or whatever!

Best Buddies

Steven and Connie love spending time together. What would you rather do with your best bud? Circle your choices below, and then make plans to hang with your friends and do this stuff!

Eat Cookie Cats or Eat Lion Lickers

Watch TV or Play video games

Play football or Play beach volleyball

Go to the amusement park or Go to the movies

Fight a Gem Monster or Fight a Homeworld Gem

Read a book or Play with toys

Fuse with Amethyst or Fuse with Pearl

Fly like a bird or Swim like a fish

Go to school or Go shopping

Ride a bicycle or Ride a unicycle

Door Decor

Using safety scissors, cut out this door hanger, hang it on your bedroom doorknob, and let everyone know you're training to become a Crystal Gem. When you want some peace and quiet, hang it with the other side facing out.

Crystal Gem in Training!

Family Time

There are lots of kinds of families. Some are big, some are small. But what matters most is that family members love and take care of one another when needed. Sometimes even friends can be as close as family! Tell us about your family below.

How many people are in your family?

_____

Do you all live together in the same house or are you all spread out?

_____

What are some activities you like to do with your family?

_____

Which of your friends are as close as family?

_____

What kind of family do you want to have when you grow up?

_____

Family Meal

One of the best things a family can do t
around the table and eat a meal. Even though
don't need to eat, Steven likes to make food
Talk to your family, and decide on a meal you
Plan out the menu below. Then, use the conv
on the next page to have a good conversation

Menu

Main Course:

....

Side Dish:

....

Dessert:

....

Drink:

....

What is something that you did well today?

. . . .

. . . .

How did someone help you?

. . . .

. . . .

What do you like about yourself today?

. . . .

. . . .

What made you happy today?

. . . .

. . . .

What made you sad today?

. . . .

. . . .

What are you excited about?

. . . .

. . . .

Family History

Steven's mother, Rose Quartz, had to give up her physical form so that Steven could be born, which means he never got to meet her. But he loves hearing stories about her from the Crystal Gems and his dad, Greg. Write down memories you have of your family members. They can be fun activities you did together, talks you had, or funny things that happened. Then ask your parents, grandparents, or an older sibling the questions on the next page, and record their answers so you can remember them forever.

What did you like to do when you were my age?

....

....

What's your favorite memory of being a kid?

....

....

What kind of house did you live in?

....

....

What was your favorite food?

....

....

What's something funny that happened to you when you were younger?

....

....

Congratulations

You've made it! After completing the activities in this book, you're now ready to help the Crystal Gems save the world! Using safety scissors, cut out the certificate on the next page to show the world you're an honorary Crystal Gem!

This is to certify that

(your name)

is an honorary
Crystal Gem

as of

Pearl AMETHYST

Garnet

(date)

Page 17
Fusion Confusion
1:d; 2:e; 3:b; 4:c; 5:a; 6:f

Page 18
Garnet Quiz
1:c; 2:a; 3:c; 4:b

Page 19
Pearl Quiz
1:d; 2:a; 3:c; 4:b

Page 20
Amethyst Quiz
1:b; 2:b; 3:d; 4:c

Page 21
Steven Quiz
1:c; 2:a; 3:b; 4:b

Page 24
The Bits! The Bits!

Pages 28–29
Do or Do Nut

Hmm, we'll review your answers and get back to you.

Page 31
The U Stor

Pages 32–35
Who's Who: Human Edition
1. Greg Universe
2. Connie
3. Fryman
4. Mr. Smiley
5. Onion
6. Mayor Dewey
7. Jenny
8. Lars
9. Dr. Maheswaran
10. Peedee Fryman
11. Buck Dewey
12. Mr. Maheswaran
13. Jamie
14. Kofi
15. Sadie

Page 36
Connie Quiz
1:c; 2:a; 3:d; 4:a

Page 37
Greg Quiz
1:c; 2:b; 3:d; 4c

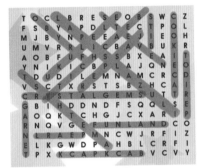